MW01644820

Published in the United States by
Gloucester Press, in 1979

Originated and produced by
The Archon Press Ltd
70, Old Compton Street
London W1V 5PA

First published in
Great Britain 1979 by
Hamish Hamilton Children's Books Ltd
Garden House, 57-59 Long Acre
London WC2E 9JL

Printed in Great Britain by
W S Cowell Ltd
Butter Market, Ipswich

Certain illustrations originally published in
The Closer Look Series

Library of Congress
Catalog Card Number: 79-63211
ISBN: 0-531-03444-5
ISBN 0-531-03408-9 (Lib.Bdg.)

Birds

Consultant editor
Henry Pluckrose

Illustrated by
John Rignall, Maurice Wilson

Gloucester Press · New York · Toronto · 1979

All birds have one thing in common: feathers. Feathers are what make birds different from all other animals.

Cuckoo

These birds are all common in Europe.
They live in woodlands and hedges.
Some birds eat nuts, seeds, and berries; others eat insects and small animals, such as mice and shrews.
Woodpeckers and nuthatches tap the bark of trees with their pointed beaks.
They are searching for insects.
You can hear them tapping from far away.
Some birds, such as willow warblers, build their nests close to the ground; others nest in bushes and shrubs.
Woodpeckers make holes in tree trunks in which to lay their eggs.

Cuckoos lay their eggs in the nests of other birds.
A baby cuckoo pushes the other eggs and baby birds out of the nest.

Willow warbler

Great spotted woodpecker
Treecreeper
Jay
Nuthatch
Song thrush
Chaffinch
Wren
Coal tit

Tawny owl

Owls hunt at night, and they can hear and see so well that even on the darkest night they are able to find their prey.
The merest rustle of a mouse will show an owl where to find it.
Owls have soft feathers all over their bodies so they fly silently.

Osprey

Birds of prey are very beautiful hunters. They have powerful claws with which they catch and kill animals and fish. Some even kill and eat other birds. Their curved beaks are for tearing their food into pieces.

The osprey is very good at catching fish. Its feet are designed to carry them.

Peregrine falcon plucking a bluejay

When birds of prey spot a small animal, they plummet quickly down onto it. The harpy eagle (opposite) is the biggest eagle and lives in South American jungles. It catches quite big animals, like monkeys.

Common buzzard

Birds of prey have excellent eyesight and can spot small animals from high in the sky

Buzzards are much smaller birds of prey than harpy eagles. This one is catching a rabbit.

Harpy eagle

Albatrosses are clumsy on land but graceful in the air. They glide without moving their wings.

Young pelicans take half digested food from the mouths of their parents.

Some birds spend most of their time far out at sea and only come on land to nest. Frigate birds can soar for hours at a time. They rarely go in the water, but snatch fish from the surface or from other birds.

Male frigate birds blow up the red pouches on their throats to attract females.

Male frigate bird

Many birds that live on open plains fly rarely and some big ones cannot fly at all. These birds have long, powerful legs. They can run away fast from their enemies. Birds that live in the desert have dull feathers so they cannot easily be seen.

Ostriches are the biggest birds of all. Male ostriches are taller than people. Ostriches live in the dry, open areas of central Africa in flocks of 10 to 50 birds. They defend themselves against enemies by kicking with their powerful legs.

Penguins live in large groups in the Antarctic. They cannot fly, but they swim very well. Their wings have developed into flippers. Adult penguins have stiff, closely packed feathers to protect them from the cold. Baby penguins are left in the care of a few adults while the others catch food in the sea.

These baby emperor penguins have fluffy feathers.

It is hard to see snowy owls against the Arctic snow because they have white feathers. They eat lemmings, Arctic hares, mice and birds, like the Arctic ptarmigan.

Snowy owl

Here are some of the brilliant birds that are found in tropical forests.

Many of the birds that live in tropical forests have very bright plumage. Some of the most beautiful birds, the birds of paradise, live in forests in New Guinea. The males do fantastic displays to attract the females which have duller feathers. Many tropical birds scream and squawk. Their voices do not match their looks.

Parrot

The male great bird of paradise dances on a branch to attract females.

Quetzals are found in the rain forests of Mexico and Central America. Aztec and Mayan Indians used to worship them as gods of the air. Quetzals are very bright green, but they are well hidden in the leafy jungle. Their feathers are very soft and fluffy. The females are less brilliant than the males and do not have long tail feathers.

Wild budgerigars (parakeets) are green, but tame ones may be blue, white and yellow.

In the breeding season male quetzals grow extra long tail feathers.

Male quetzal

Ocellated turkey

The ocellated turkey lives in Mexico. It spreads its tail and shows the beautiful patterns on its feathers.

Goldcrests are the smallest birds in Europe. They are slightly bigger than in the picture. In America there is a very similar bird called a golden-crowned kinglet. Goldcrests hang their tiny nests made of moss, cobwebs and feathers from the branches of fir trees.

Humming-birds are so tiny and brilliant that they look like jewels. They can fly sideways and even backwards. Their name comes from the humming sound made by their wings when they beat them fast. Humming-birds hover in front of flowers feeding on nectar and tiny insects.

Humming-bird

Crane

Many birds, like swallows, breed in one place and migrate to warm areas in winter. How they know when and where to go is a mystery, but every year they make the trip. Arctic terns fly halfway round the world in six weeks – further than any migrating birds.

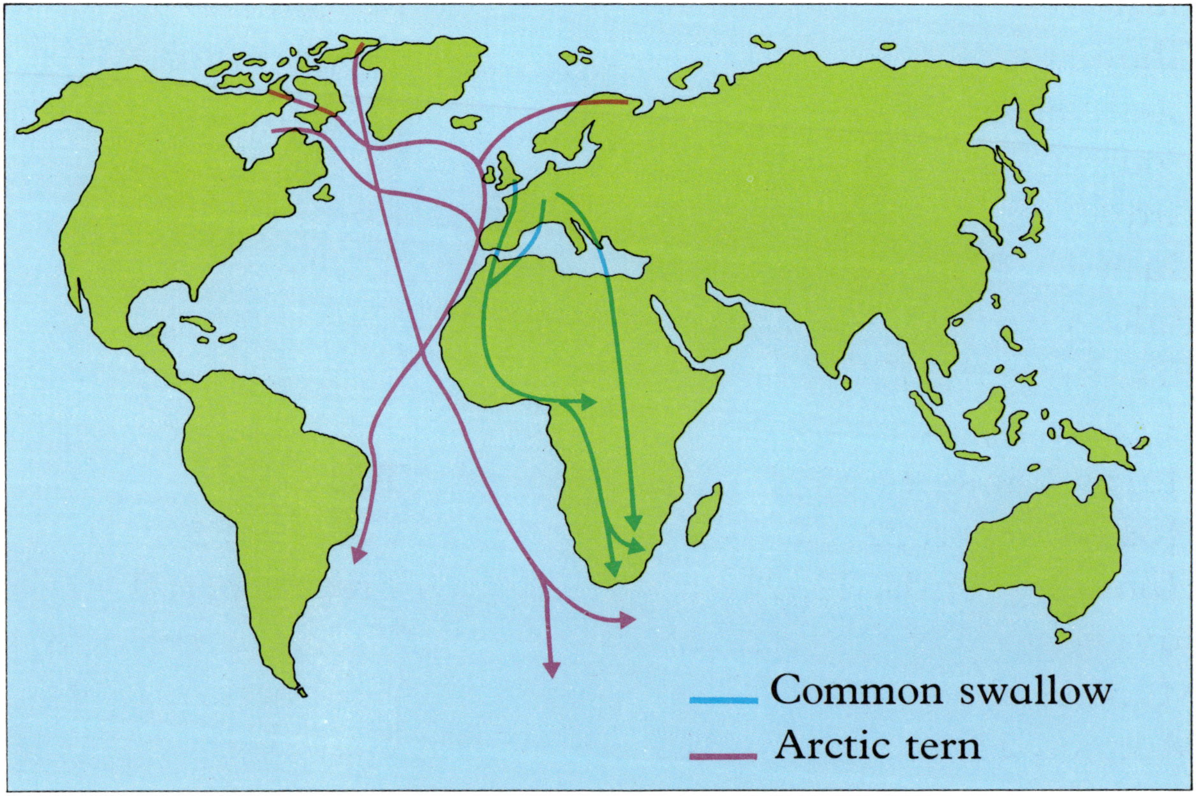

Common swallow
Arctic tern

Index